1.

BAREFOOT IN THE NIGHT

For the ones who cannot be tamed,
who run with the wind and chase the stars.

Her silhouette moved in the sunset
a rebellion of crimson light
and I knew then
what I'd always known—
she'd never be mine to keep
but we had at least this fading dance.

Some souls shine where the world forgets to look.

Some girls are born to run—
wild horses in endless fields—
we chase them but never catch them.

Her wild is
a melody—
learn the
notes or
lose the
song.

She was a flicker in the woods
a flame dancing through the pines
and I chased her glow
till the trees swallowed us whole.

He fell in love with the untamed truth
that she was an ocean
a cool wind urging him
toward unnamed lands
and untold stories.

Some girls
are born with
wildfires in
their veins.

The world was her stage
and she sang and danced the part.

She was a comet in my quiet sky
blazing through the dark
leaving trails of dust and magic
for me to follow through the night.

She leaned into the storm
and laughed at the thunder
as if it were an old friend.

Life's too short for sober shadows
so we drank in the moonlight
and let them dance
to the music of our hearts.

FEAR IS A
THIEF—
DON'T LET IT
STEAL
YOUR WILD.

Speak your truth
loud and unshaken
be so powerful
they have no choice but to listen.

Some hearts are rivers—
deep and wild and never still
forever flowing to the music they hear.

Some hearts are oceans—
too deep to chart
too wild to keep.

Some girls are storms dressed up in sunlight.

Sometimes you
just need to
stop and
smell the
rosé.

She was a bird
born to dance in the wind
but always the world
tried to hold her back
and keep her on the ground.

But she never stopped.

Always rising again and again
unfurling her wings to the sky
her heart to the wind.
And the universe fell in love with her
as it always did when souls danced.

Her heart and the stars were her guides
leading her ever on
toward the life that called her
and she followed them, smiling
knowing everything she dreamed of
was right along this path.

Her eyes were a forest at dusk
deep with secrets and soft with promise
a place I'd wander
and never want to leave.

She was a mystery to me
and at first, I tried to solve her
like everyone does—
but some mysteries
are not there to be solved.
They are there to be loved.

We sipped whiskey under the bruising sky
toasting to this heaven that we'd made on Earth
and I knew then—
this was our forever
fleeting as it was.

2.

LOVE & BEAUTIFUL RUIN

For those who love recklessly, who give their hearts.

Skinny dipping in December—
the reckless hymn of hearts too in love to freeze.

A
Some souls
flicker like
candles
too tender to
burn through
life alone.
A

She ran barefoot through the dusk
a shadow chasing the light
and I followed
lost in her reckless grace.

I could spend a lifetime spilling ink
and never write the whole of her.

J
Love is
the wild you
choose to
run with.
J

In the greatest love, we discover who we really are.

I have never felt more alive
than the first few days in love.

What a beautiful thing it is
to fall in love and uncover
all the weird things
that make you perfect
for each other.

Love isn't worth suffering for—
love is worth fighting for.

Watch the change that occurs in a relationship
when you stop taking and start giving.

Life is the art of acting normal long enough
to find someone weird like you.

Nothing re-prioritizes your life faster
than falling head over heels in love.

Fall slowly
into good love
and quickly out
of bad.

Nothing compares to young love—
the discovery of something so new
yet so ancient
as if in this moment
ours is the first love
the universe has ever known
and the last.

What I loved most in her
was a deep desire to be better.
I was in love with this person
and in love with who she would one day be.

In relationships both must always grow and move
for if one grows and moves forward
and one does not
one day they will wake to find
they are no longer in the same room.

You've kissed off more than you can chew.

Don't put too much pressure on the search
many of the best love stories started with a stumble—
accidents in airports and coffee shops.
It could happen today.

She had lived so many lives
in this short life of hers.
She was constantly shedding
and reinventing who she was and why
and I knew it would always be the same
but hoped I could hold on
for this short while
before we were shed
like everybody else.

I will send your ghost shimmering
down the ages of history
as poetry on a page.
You will live on
I swear
as words and ink on parchment
until dust steals you away.

I will be a stone in the river for you, my love.
There for you through ups and downs
to crash upon
unmoving
and the world will rush by us
but you will always find me.
I will be where you left me.

Our bodies may go
but our atoms
find each other
again and again
until the end of time.

To love truly is to risk being shattered
into a million pieces
but what a beautiful way to fall apart.

The trick to a love poem
is being with someone
who makes the words write themselves.

Her skin held the salty kiss of a thousand tides—
every wave a story
I longed to drown in
a thousand times.

Love is a leap you take without wings
and learn that falling is just another word for flying.

He loved her softly, at first
like the dawn.
Then like a burning sun
that would never fade.

We danced on the rooftop
the city lights our chandeliers
her laughter
the only music I'd ever need.

She was a spark in the falling snow
a bold defiance against the cold
and I warmed my hands
on her glow.

Love is a secret whispered in that endless space
between heartbeats.

Some loves are stars—
brief, bright, and burning—
gone before you blink.

We danced in the rain-soaked streets
barefoot and untamed
our shadows tangling
like colored paint
too mixed now to ever be apart.

Love is a fragrance
that lingers long after the flowers have withered
and the petals have fallen
reminding us always
of the beauty that once was.

The greatest expression of love is not found in words
but in actions
in the way we show up for each other
day after day.

Love is the art of accepting a person
for exactly who they are
where they are
and where they are going to be.

Love is a bridge that connects two hearts
even and especially
when they are thousands of miles apart.

you don't find love
you become it
it weaves you into
who you are.

To love is to feel the warmth of the sun
and chill of the wind
all at once, in a grand tingle
of pins and needles.

The true meaning of love is not found in grand gestures
but in the small and simple moments
that fill our lives with joy.

Love is the glue that binds us together
even when everything else seems to fall apart.

A well-hidden note often holds more power
than a bouquet of flowers.

And so—wrapped in chaos and wonder of new love—
she surrendered herself
her heart given willingly
to the whims of fate.

In love, the heart becomes a garden where the most beautiful flowers can bloom.

Love is
a bridge
to heaven.

Love is alchemy
transforming hearts to gold
and souls to magic.

Love is not always gentle—
sometimes it is a wildfire
consuming everything in its path
leaving nothing but ash and smoke.
But even then
we crave its warmth.

I have loved and lost
more times than I can count
but I will not give up
for it is the one thing
I've come to realize
that makes life worth living.

I used to think
that love was a destination
a happy place
to arrive at
and settle in forever.
But I know now
that it's a journey, a cause to fight for
an adventure that takes work, and effort, and building.
But it's worth it in the end—
I was right about that at least.

Sometimes the greatest act of love
is to let go
to release the past
and make space for a new beginning.

In love, always think long term.
Will this fight matter when we are old folks
playing crib in a retirement home?
It seldom does.

I met a monk once.
I asked him of love,
"How can one be compassionate
and not taken advantage of?"
He smiled.
"Never be a doormat," he said.
"That's not helping anyone.
Better to be a door
and let them go."

3.

CRUMPLED LEAVES

For the ones who have lost, who have left, who are learning to begin again.

Loss is the shadow that follows us through life
but also the light
that guides us
to help us fall more deeply into love
with every moment that we have.

Love is the echo of a laugh you can't forget—
it stays with you forever like a gentle fading sunset.

Tomorrow is the
gift of trying
again where
you left off.

I lingered in her absence
a ghost of her love
haunting the hollow chambers of my heart—
day and night, near or far.

Forgiveness is not forgetting
not excusing the hurt—
it is setting down the weight
of anger and resentment
so you can be free.

Love withers when it dies
like a rose wilting from the frost—
it tries to live, it wants to
but some things must die for others to live.

Life is a never-ending dance
where the music never stops
and the drinks never run dry—
until, of course, they do.

Our hearts break
again and again
but always they mend
making us stronger
in those broken
places.

She was a melody in the silence
a song I'd forever hum
on those lonely nights
long after the music faded.

The sunset told her that endings can be beautiful too.

Sometimes

the bravest thing
we can do
is be gentle
with ourselves
slow down
and allow our souls
the time they need
to heal.

Her footsteps echoed on the cobblestones—
a rhythm of restless dreams—
and I trailed behind
lost in her song
dancing forever on the starlit stones.

Love is the echo of a heartbeat you will never forget.

Love is the chaos
you choose to
dance in.

She held the dawn in her hands—
a fragile promise of new beginnings—
and let it spill over into a world
still sleeping.

Leaving him was like taking off
a backpack of heavy stones—
each step grew lighter
and the road more bright
and deep within
a little spark of hope began
to burn her back to life.

Anger is often grief in disguise—
ask yourself what you are truly mourning.

Love is the
risk of losing
your heart
to find another.

Love is not always about staying—
sometimes it's about knowing when to leave.

I remember your touch
cool and calm against my skin
gentle in a way that made the world pause.
It's something I miss so much.
And though you are far away
my love for you burns steady
a constant flame
even in a storm.

The pain of loss is a testament to the depth of our love—
the more we loved
the more we hurt.

The tears we shed for the ones we've lost
are the price we pay
for the joy they brought into our lives.

The greatest lie in the world is that our partners are ours to keep.

In loss

we learn the value
of what we had
and the emptiness
of what remains.

Loss is the wound that never truly heals
but with time
it becomes the scar that reminds us of the love
we once held dear.

Her tears were a river
flowing from her soul
and they washed away the sadness
and healed her heart with the currents.
All the sadness was forgotten
as they were carried ever further down the
stream.

Hope is a powerful thing
for in darkness
all it takes
is the slightest glimmer
to remind us of the
brightness that
could be.

She was on the first few pages of her life's grand story.
So many false starts
thrown in a wastebasket
but this one was it
she felt it in her bones.
This was her forever story unfolding.

You can fall in love with someone who doesn't
know themselves
but you can't be in love with someone who
doesn't love themselves.

4.

WHEN STARS WHISPER

For those who see magic in the stars, in the moon,
in the spaces between words.

Like a bird on the wind
I dance
wild and untamed
a whisper of freedom against the sky.

The world pulls
but
I do not fall.

With every beat of my heart
I taste the sweet breeze
singing love songs to the open air.

Her soul was a prism
of lights and color
reflecting a different part of me
with every look.
In rainbows and lavenders
she made me see myself anew
and the infinite possibilities
of who I could still become.

The stars leaned closer when she spoke
as if they craved her words
and I listened
a fool for her cosmic poetry.

The sea roared her name
and she answered with a laugh
diving into waves
that mirrored her soul.

We are all flowers and together a garden.

We spend our adult lives carefully hiding
that wild bird within us
that wants to fly high and far
and dance in meadows with naked feet.

I once met a monk
and he said to me,
"Don't forget that all this busy
all this stress
all these worries are yours.
At any point
you can choose
a simple life
and be free."

She brought sunrises into my life—
I'd seen them before, but not like she saw them.
She saw colors I had never seen
like it was the first time
our Earth had seen the sun
and might also be the last.
And that's the way
she was with life—
grateful and astonished
by all of its miracles.

I've walked through deserts
and felt the scorching sun
but it's the times I've been lost
when the map was only sky
and the road was only dust
that I truly began
to find myself.

The ocean reminds us
that even the most violent storms
eventually
find their way back to calm.

Don't ever
hide the
wild truth
that is
you.

It took me a lifetime to realize
it's the small things that matter most—
the way the grass feels between your toes
or the way your hand reaches to my back
in the morning
to make sure I'm there.

We found each other in the dark times
and would go out to the desert
where the night sky was our canvas
and we painted it in shooting stars.
For the first time in life
she showed that it wasn't just the stars
that were beautiful
for the darkness between them made them shine.

The present moment is the only one we truly have.
Let us learn to cherish it
for it is where our lives unfold.

She stood beneath the old wise tree
whispering to its roots
and the branches trembled
with the weight of her dreams.

There is a place within us all
where our soul
meets the stars
and we are reminded
that we are all made of magic.

life is a symphony

of highs and lows

so keep on dancing

until the music slows

For all of my life
I have thought
I am not enough
but as life went on
I began to listen
to what the universe
was whispering all along.
I am made of stardust
and the universe
does not create anything
that is not perfectly enough already.

We come from a long line of survivors.
From the beginning
we are the ones who made it.

The stars above me
are a reminder of my dreams
a reminder that anything is possible
if I have the courage to reach for the sky.

Some souls are too vast
to fit in a single sky.
That was hers
and I would spend a lifetime uncovering
the universe of her.

The wind whispers secrets to me
in a language only my soul understands.
A reminder that sometimes the greatest wisdom
comes from within.

The night is a mystery
shrouded in cloud and shadow.
I crave and fear its lonely secrets
for even in that darkest dark
there is beauty to be found
if only we look closely enough
and listen for its silent song.

The sky was a canvas
painted in pinks and golds
and the setting sun
warmed our battered souls.
We remembered that day
the beauty that surrounded us
as if our hearts were dipped
in honey once more.

Her shadow stretched across the sand—
a promise of endless stories and adventures—
and I walked beside it now, hand in hand
thankful for the company.

Her heart
beats in colors
the world has
no name for.

Her boots left prints in the sand—
each step a quiet rebellion
against a world too small for her.

Her hair smelled of campfires and nights under the stars—
a girl I'd chase through a thousand summers.

She was the kind of wild that made the other stars jealous—
she would dance
and they would dim
and I would smile at the universe
dancing so close to the brightest star that ever shone.

She was the trail
I'd walk
without light
trusting her steps
to the edge
of all I knew.

We floated down French rivers
wine soaking in our veins
crickets humming as the sun dipped low—
this was our heaven
etched forever in fleeting summers.

I measure
my happiness
in laughs
and wine.

Nature is God's muse, allowing artists to simply forget their imaginations, and instead paint the truth of what they see.

The stars are old stories
raining down on us
in memories of skies long ago
and we stand grateful
for their light.

5.

SINGING THROUGH STORMS

For those who are still finding themselves, still learning how to stand in their own light.

Scars are the stars of your untold story.

In love, the greatest gift is providing space for
someone to be their truest self.

The little children we were show up again and again, always at the worst of times.

*There's something
in all ways magic
about you just the
way you're you.*

It is wise to watch what we dislike in others—
it is so often something we dislike in ourselves.

Sometimes the greatest gift we can give to a loved one is healing ourselves first.

Love yourself enough
to never let someone hurt you twice.

Promise me
you won't leave this world
with all those words left inside you.

Letting go of someone and moving on doesn't mean you don't honor them and what you had—it just means you honor yourself enough to know that chapter is complete.

My whole life changed when I stopped resenting the scared little child inside me and started giving them the unconditional care and understanding they never received.

Before we heal, we must first accept
that we have been hurt.

It's a great freedom the day we realize
it's okay to not feel okay.
Happiness is a moment, not a constant
and being sad is a necessary part of being happy.

Look for the people with old friends and new.
Be wary of the ones with only new.

Sometimes the best way
to battle an overwhelming emotion
is to soak within it for a moment.
Feel it truly and deeply, honor it and thank it
for making you feel at all
and let it pass by
as it always does.

Some of us
don't fear
the storm—
we are the
storm.

Our greatest challenges are often our greatest
opportunities for growth and transformation.

I am not just this body that you see.
I am fear and dreams and flesh and bones.
I am futures and pasts
young and old—
a universe within myself that is
constantly changing, ever expanding.

The world crumpled me again and again
like a fallen leaf
but within that mulch of youth
lay hidden seeds
that slowly grew
into an oak tree
to stand as I am
against the winds of change
forever reaching
toward the blue sky of hope.

Happiness isn't given
it is earned
on the treacherous journey
to finding oneself.

When healing, there is no destination to arrive at—
just a safer place beyond the tears
to live beside your scars.

What a gift to give yourself
to see the worn road of old patterns
so well-traveled and familiar
and then take an unfamiliar turn away
toward the orchards of your new self.

Some girls are storms
that you'll never outrun, nor should you try.
They'll swallow you up and spin you around
to leave you danced and dazed
with a smile on your face
and a kiss mark on your cheek—
a reminder to you it was real.

The greatest gift you could give yourself
is to stop trying to convince your partner
of all the wrongs you see
and just leave
and live in rightness and truth
somewhere else
with someone else.

She wove her dreams into the breeze—
a fragile thread of hope—
and let it drift
where the wind would take her.

Love her flaws—
the ones she so carefully hides—
that's where the magic is.

Fear is just a shadow—
step out of the light and watch it shrink to nothing.

She carved her truth in the sand
watching the tide take it away again and again
smiling at the magic
of letting go.

Her tears fell like rain on the dry earth
and from them grew a garden.
Vines and flowers of strength and power
that no one could uproot.

Her courage is quiet—
a whisper in the dark
that shakes the earth
for all that feel it.

Her voice was a sparrow—
small but unbroken
singing through storms
to call the sun home.

Growth happens when you realize
the old story you've told yourself
is no longer who you are.

In the right
love and the
wrong love
we still grow.

There is free love and caged love—
one bird flies
and the other has forgotten how
but it still dreams of the sky when it closes its eyes.

You are allowed to outgrow the people who kept you small.

The greatest adventure
is not where we go
but the people we become
when we come back.

Sometimes fighting for someone is giving them space to fight for themselves.

Some souls
shine
brightest
when the
world goes
dark.

And so she left
on a journey without and within
to find herself and lose herself again and again.

Healing is not a straight line—it's a spiral that returns you to old wounds with new strength.

Healing is not about becoming someone new—
it's about remembering who you've always been.

Sometimes healing means letting go of the future you thought you wanted.

True joy is not the absence of sorrow
but the courage to hold both joy and sorrow at once.

The greatest obstacle in life is not what lies ahead but the fear of taking the first step.

I am forever a work in progress
a painting never finished
a sculpture half done
but with every stroke of the brush or setting of clay
I discover something new about myself
that I didn't know before
and I become more complete.

I am an apple tree
growing every day, sunny and rainy alike.
Sometimes blooming, sometimes withering
but always reaching toward the light
and digging roots down.
All I hope
is that I leave this little meadow
better than it was without me.

We must all learn
to love ourselves again
to embrace our flaws
to celebrate our strengths
and fall madly and deeply
head over heels in love
with who we are, who we were
and who we will one day be.

I am not
the person I was or will be
I have shed this skin a thousand times
and will again.
So do not guess you know me
who I've been, or who I will be
for I wasn't the same person then
and I won't be the same person you meet tomorrow.

My mind is a grand labyrinth
of thoughts and emotions
sometimes chaos, sometimes confusion
but always true.
A reflection of my humanity
and my great imperfect imbalance
of being human.

My body is a temple
of strength and resilience—
each scar a testament
to my ability to endure
to keep going.
I am a warrior.

It took me a lifetime to realize
that my scars are not flaws—
they are a constellation
of the long journey
that brought me here
and made me who I am.

The most powerful form of love
is the love we create for ourselves.

Our power lies
not in our ability to control the external world
but in our capacity
to control our own minds within it.

She was a force, fierce and unbreakable
forged in the fires of pain and youth.
But the scared little girl was grown now
leaving instead a woman
who knew exactly who she was and why.
Who took that little girl by the hand
and whispered in her ear,
"We are safe now, you and I.
There is no man or monster left
strong enough to defeat us."

There is a quiet freedom
in realizing
you don't have to convince them,
you don't have to change their mind—
you can just leave.

Don't fear the storm
for it's always after the heaviest rains
that the real growth begins.

What does a poet have left in them
but all the words jumbled in a million ways
in the never-ending search
for something beautiful.

Break free, my love—
the cage was
never locked.

ABOUT THE AUTHOR

Atticus is a *New York Times* bestselling author of *Love Her Wild, The Dark Between Stars, The Truth About Magic, LVOE., Spark: The One-Sentence Journal,* and *LVOE.: Volume II.* He is a storyteller, traveler, and observer. He spends much of his life exploring the world. He loves the ocean, the desert, and playing with words. After losing a close friend, Atticus made a choice to remain forever anonymous, preferring instead to "send love from the shadows."

Visit him on Instagram at @atticuspoetry.

The authorised representative in the EEA is Simon and Schuster Netherlands BV, Herculesplein 96 3584 AA Utrecht, Netherlands. (info@simonandschuster.nl)

Andrews McMeel Publishing
a division of Andrews McMeel Universal
1130 Walnut Street, Kansas City, Missouri 64106

www.andrewsmcmeel.com

26 27 28 29 30 TE2 10 9 8 7 6 5 4 3 2 1

ISBN: 978-1-5248-9541-9

Library of Congress Control Number: 2026935606

Editor: Danys Mares
Art Director: Julie Barnes
Production Editor: Elizabeth A. Garcia
Production Manager: Julia Skalla
Creative Director: Ashley Chase

Cover art courtesy of Atticus Publishing, LLC, created with the assistance of MidJourney and Reve AI, February 12, 2026.

FSC
www.fsc.org
MIX
Paper | Supporting responsible forestry
FSC® C016973